ENGLiSH TOWN

FOR
EVERYONE

BOOK

5

Contents

Characters

Theme Song

Hello Song

Hello, everyone.
Hello, teacher!
Hello, friends!

Let's have fun together.
We'll have a good time.

Are you ready to start?
We're ready!

Here we go!

Goodbye Song

Did you have fun?

It's time to say goodbye.
See you next time!
See you next time!

Did you enjoy the class?
Yes! We had a fun time!
Yes! We had a fun time!

See you later! See you later!
Goodbye. Goodbye.

Bye! Bye!

I'm in the Fourth Grade

Let's Talk

A. Look, listen, and repeat.

6

B. Listen and repeat.

I'm in the **first** grade.

① **1st**
first

② **2nd**
second

③ **3rd**
third

④ **4th**
fourth

C. Listen, point, and say.

What grade are you in?
I'm in the _____ grade.

Let's Learn

A. Listen and chant.

How are you doing?

I'm fine. I'm fine.

What grade are you in?

I'm in the third grade, the third grade.

How are you doing?

I'm great. I'm great.

What grade are you in?

I'm in the fourth grade, the fourth grade.

B. Read, look, and match.

① A: What grade are you in?
   B: I'm in the third grade.

② A: What grade are you in?
   B: I'm in the first grade.

③ A: What grade are you in?
   B: I'm in the second grade.

2nd

3rd

1st

C. Guess and write. Ask and answer.

GRADE | first   second   third   fourth   fifth   sixth

① fifth

② _____

③ _____

④ _____

⑤ _____

⑥ _____

A: What grade are you in?
B: I'm in the third grade.

D. Play the "Dice Game."

- Throw a dice. Then answer the question using the number on it.

Round	Me	Friend
1		
2		
3		
Total		

- 1st grade
- 2nd grade
- 3rd grade
- 4th grade
- 5th grade
- 6th grade

Add up the number of grades. The student who gets more points wins.

Lesson 2

Does This School Have a Library?

Let's Talk

A. Look, listen, and repeat.

Act It Out

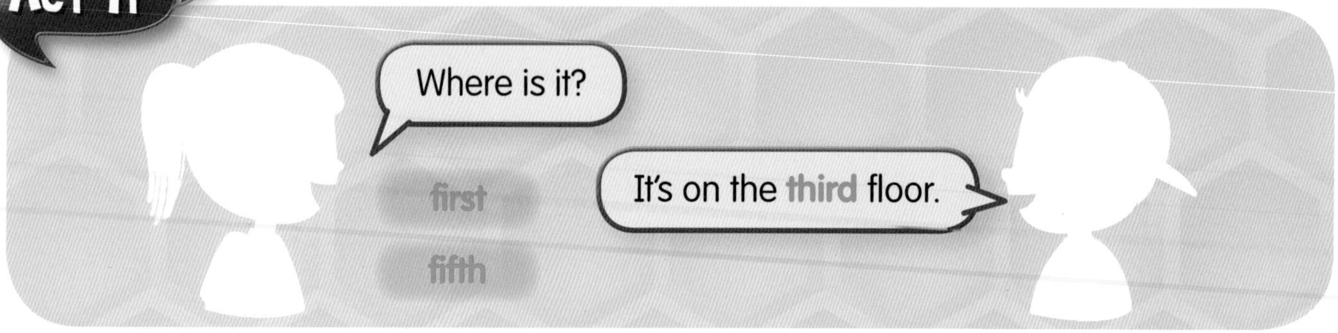

B. Listen and repeat.

Does this school have a **cafeteria** ?

①
cafeteria

②
gym

③
music room

④
science lab

C. Listen, point, and say.

Does this school have a _____ ?
– Yes, it does.

①
♪ MUSIC ROOM

②

③

④

5

Let's Learn

A. Listen and chant.

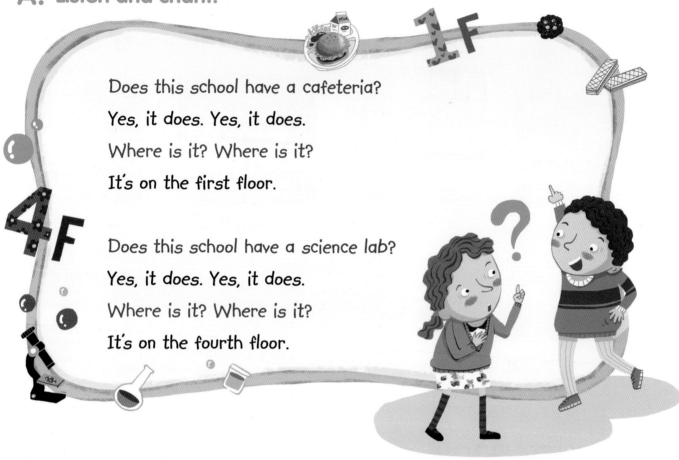

Does this school have a cafeteria?
Yes, it does. Yes, it does.
Where is it? Where is it?
It's on the first floor.

Does this school have a science lab?
Yes, it does. Yes, it does.
Where is it? Where is it?
It's on the fourth floor.

B. Listen, look, and match.

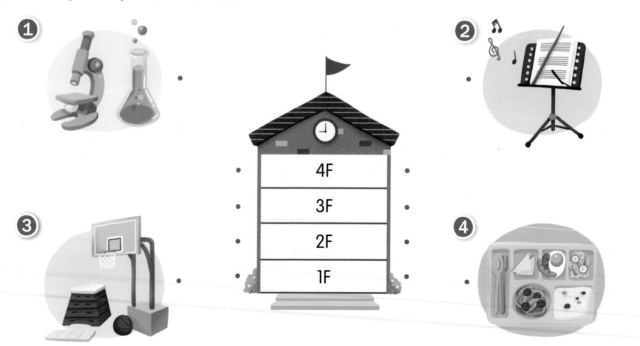

4F
3F
2F
1F

e-learning

A: Does this school have a **music room**?

B: Yes, it does. / No, it doesn't.

C. Ask, answer, and check.

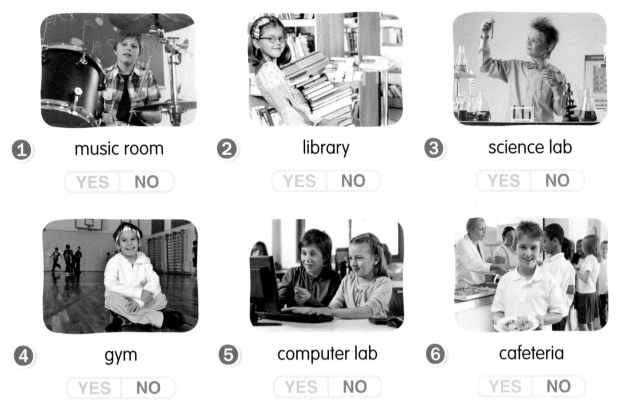

1 music room   YES | NO

2 library   YES | NO

3 science lab   YES | NO

4 gym   YES | NO

5 computer lab   YES | NO

6 cafeteria   YES | NO

A: Does our school have a computer lab?
B: Yes, it does.

D. Write. Ask and answer.

- Write the school facilities. Then ask and answer about your school.

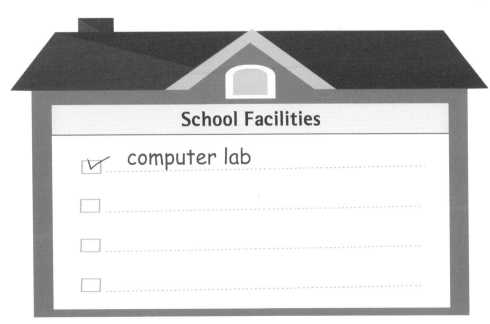

School Facilities

☑ computer lab

☐ ....

☐ ....

☐ ....

Lesson 3 — A New Friend

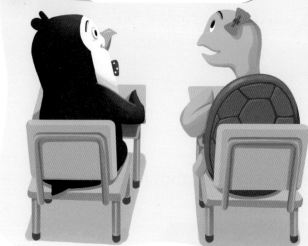

A. Look, listen, and repeat.

B. Listen again and write the number in.

1. Nice to meet you, too.
2. Really? That's great.
3. Hi, Paul. What grade are you in?
4. Yes, it does. It's on the third floor.

14

Bibble Paula Paul

C. Read and circle True or False.

1. Bibble is Paula's old friend.   True   False
2. There is no cafeteria in the school.   True   False
3. Paula has a brother.   True   False
4. Paul is in the second grade.   True   False

D. Do a role-play.

Lesson 3 · 15

Let's Play

A. Listen and sing.

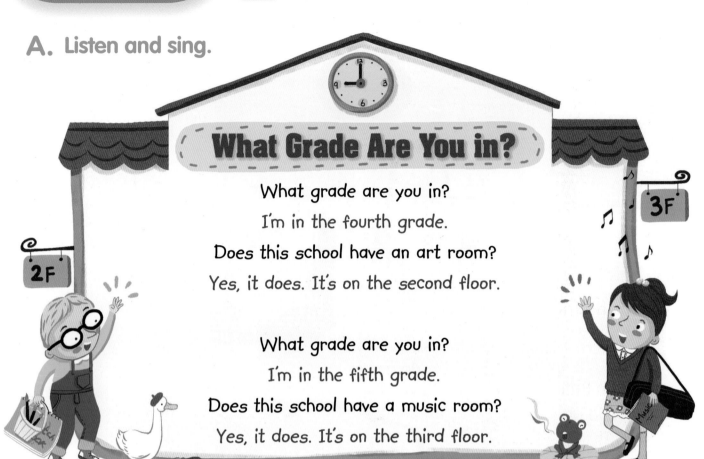

What Grade Are You in?

What grade are you in?
I'm in the fourth grade.
Does this school have an art room?
Yes, it does. It's on the second floor.

What grade are you in?
I'm in the fifth grade.
Does this school have a music room?
Yes, it does. It's on the third floor.

B. Play a board game.

Does this school have a science lab?

START

FINISH

I'm in the fifth grade.

e-learning

First Floor vs. Ground Floor

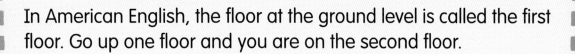

In American English, the floor at the ground level is called the first floor. Go up one floor and you are on the second floor.

In British English, the same floor is always called the ground floor.
Go up one floor and you are on the first floor.
The floor above that is the second floor, and so on.
Do you want to go up the second floor in the UK?
Then you have to go up the third floor.

Second Floor

First Floor

CHECK IT OUT

US

First Floor

Ground Floor

UK

1. What is the floor at ground level in American English called?

2. What is the floor above the ground level in British English called?

How Do You Go to School?

Let's Talk

A. Look, listen, and repeat.

Good morning, Thomas.

Good morning.

You're good at inline skating.

Thank you.

How do you go to school?

I go to school by bike.

Here we go!

ACT IT OUT

Good morning.

Good morning.

evening

night

B. Listen and repeat.

I go to school **by bike** .

①

by bike

②

by bus

③

by subway

④

on foot

C. Listen, point, and say.

How do you go to school?
– I go to school _____ .

Let's Learn

A. Listen and chant.

Hello, hello. Good morning.
Hi, hi. Good morning.
How do you go to school?
I go to school on foot, on foot.

Hello, hello. Good afternoon.
Hi, hi. Good afternoon.
How do you go home?
I go home by bike, by bike.

B. Look, read, and choose.

①

A: How do you go home?

B: I go home ⓐ on foot / ⓑ by train .

②

A: How do you go to the park?

B: I go to the park ⓐ by car / ⓑ by bike .

③

A: How do you go to the museum?

B: I go to the museum ⓐ by bus / ⓑ by subway .

C. Roll the dice. Ask and answer.

①   by bike

②   on foot

③   by subway

④   by bus

⑤   by car

⑥   by boat

D. Play the "Bingo!": Write. Ask and answer.

A: How do you go to school?
B: I go to school on foot.

Transportation

- on foot
- by bus
- by car
- by boat
- by bike
- by subway

Lesson 5: Let's Save Energy

Let's Talk

A. Look, listen, and repeat.

I won't take the elevator.

watch TV

use plastic bags

That's good.

B. Listen and repeat.

Let's [plant trees] .

plant trees

recycle paper

save energy

save water

C. Listen, point, and say.

What's the message of the poster?
– Let's _____ .

Save the Earth

Let's Learn

A. Listen and chant.

What's the message of the poster?

Let's save energy. Let's save energy.

I won't take the elevator, the elevator.

That's good. That's good.

What's the message of the poster?

Let's plant trees. Let's plant trees.

I'll plant a tree tomorrow, tomorrow.

That's good. That's good.

B. Listen, look, and number.

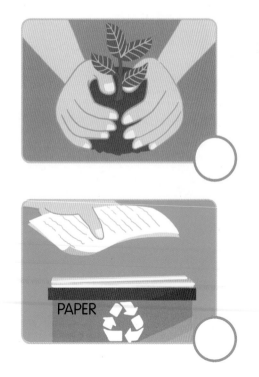

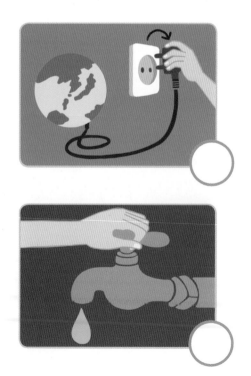

A: What's the message of the poster?

B: Let's **plant trees**.

C. Choose three posters. Ask and answer.

1 plant trees ☐

2 save the Earth ☐

3 recycle paper ☐

4 save water ☐

5 save the sea ☐

6 save energy ☐

D. Draw. Ask and answer.

A: What's the message of the poster?
B: Let's save the Earth.

My Poster

Lesson 6 Stop Global Warming

A. Look, listen, and repeat.

B. Listen again and write the number in.

1. Yes, I do.
2. We can go to school on foot.
3. Wow! You're good at painting.
4. What's the message of the poster?

Bibble Paula Teacher

C. Read and circle True or False.

1. Paula wanted to show her poster to the class.   True   False
2. Paula is good at painting.   True   False
3. The message of Paula's poster is "Let's save trees."   True   False
4. Paula will probably go to school by bus.   True   False

D. Do a role-play.

Let's Play

A. Listen and sing.

Let's Save the Earth

Oh, no! The lake is too dirty.
Let's save the lake.
What, what can we do?
We can pick up the trash in the lake.

Oh, no! The sea ice is melting.
Let's stop global warming.
What, what can we do?
We can go to school by bike.

B. Play a board game.

Let's save water.

I go to school by bus.

START

FINISH

PAPER

e-learning

Going to School around the World

Trams in San Francisco

How do the students go to school here?
Some of them go to school by tram.
Trams look like trains.

Jeepneys in the Philippines

How do the students go to school here?
Some of them go to school by jeepney.
Jeepneys look like jeeps.

Water Buses in Venice

How do the students go to school here?
Some of them go to school by water bus.
Water buses look like boats.

CHECK IT OUT

1. How do some students go to school in the Philippines?
2. How do some students go to school in Venice?

What's Your Hobby?

Let's Talk

A. Look, listen, and repeat.

ACT IT **OUT**

Do you like Sherlock Holmes?

Edison

Mozart

Yes, he's great.

B. Listen and repeat.

My hobby is **drawing pictures** .

① drawing pictures   ② reading novels   ③ riding a bike   ④ watching movies

C. Listen, point, and say.

What's your hobby?
– My hobby is _____.

Let's Learn

A. Listen and chant.

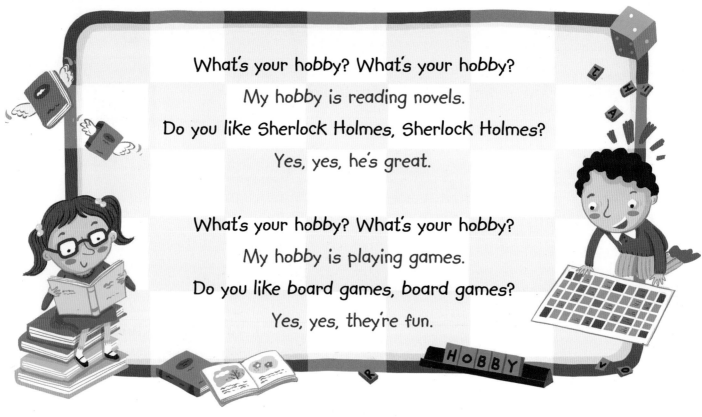

What's your hobby? What's your hobby?
My hobby is reading novels.
Do you like Sherlock Holmes, Sherlock Holmes?
Yes, yes, he's great.

What's your hobby? What's your hobby?
My hobby is playing games.
Do you like board games, board games?
Yes, yes, they're fun.

B. Read, look, and match.

1. My hobby is drawing pictures. •

2. My hobby is riding a bike. •

3. My hobby is reading novels. •

4. My hobby is watching movies. •

> A: What's your hobby?
> B: My hobby is **reading novels**.

C. Match. Ask and answer.

1
_____ novels

2
_____ soccer

3
_____ movies

reading   drawing   watching   riding   playing   taking

4
_____ pictures

5
_____ a bike

6
_____ pictures

D. Play the "Sentence Relay Game."

My **hobby is** watching movies.

 Kevin

Kevin's **hobby is** watching movies.
My **hobby is** taking pictures.

 Jenny

Kevin's **hobby is** .... Jenny's **hobby is** ....
My **hobby is** ....

 David

We Make Toy Robots

Let's Talk

A. Look, listen, and repeat.

B. Listen and repeat.

We **bake bread** .

①

②

③

④

bake bread   design clothes   make movies   make toy robots

C. Listen, point, and say.

What do you do in your club?
– We _____ .

Join Our Club

Let's Learn

A. Listen and chant.

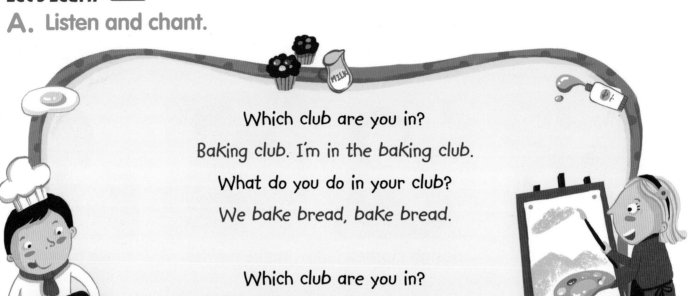

Which club are you in?
Baking club. I'm in the baking club.
What do you do in your club?
We bake bread, bake bread.

Which club are you in?
Painting club. I'm in the painting club.
What do you do in your club?
We paint pictures, paint pictures.

B. Listen, look, and circle.

① T F

② T F

③ T F

④ T F

A: What do you do in your club?

B: We **design clothes**.

C. Choose three clubs. Ask and answer.

1 design clothes ☐

2 make movies ☐

3 play tennis ☐

4 bake bread ☐

5 make toy robots ☐

6 draw cartoons ☐

D. Ask and answer. Then write.

- Ask and answer about your friends' clubs and what they do in the clubs.

A: Which club are you in?
B: I'm in the baking club.

A: What do you do in your club?
B: We bake bread and cookies.

Name	Club	Activities
• Sue	• baking club	• bake bread and cookies

Club Activities

A. Look, listen, and repeat.

B. Listen again and write the number in.

1. What's your hobby?
2. Which club are you in?
3. I didn't join a club yet.
4. I have a club meeting.

Bibble Paula

C. Read and circle True or False.

1. Bibble has a club meeting after school.   **True**   **False**
2. Bibble is in the baking club.   **True**   **False**
3. Paula's hobby is playing chess.   **True**   **False**
4. Paula wants to join the baking club.   **True**   **False**

D. Do a role-play.

A. Listen and sing.

Which Club Are You in?

Which club are you in?
I'm in the chess club.
Do you like playing chess?
Yes, I do. My hobby is playing chess.

Which club are you in?
I'm in the photo club.
Do you like taking pictures?
Yes, I do. My hobby is taking pictures.

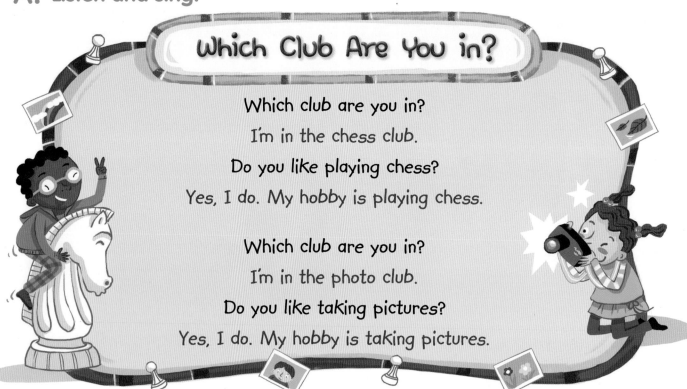

B. Play a board game.

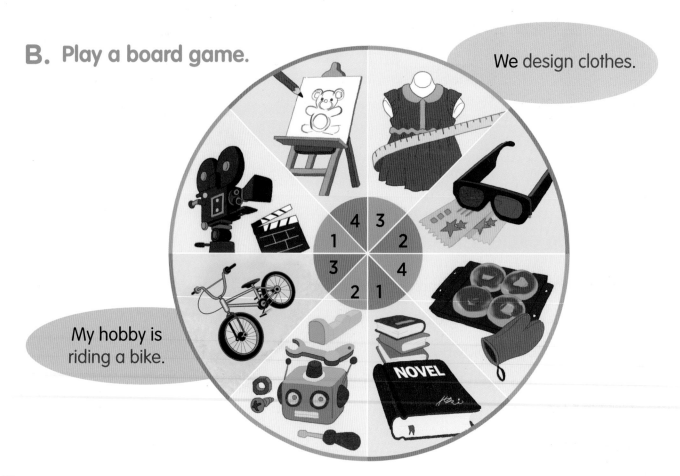

We design clothes.

My hobby is riding a bike.

New Clubs for You

Techno Sports Club

In usual sports clubs, students play sports games.
In our club, robots play soccer games.
We build our own robots.
It's a lot of fun.

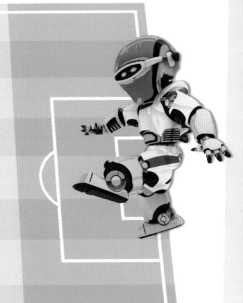

Smart Painting Club

In usual painting clubs, you draw and paint pictures on paper.
In our club, we draw and paint pictures with our tablet PCs.
We don't need to buy paper or paint.
It's amazing.

CHECK IT OUT

1. What do robots do in the Techno Sports Club?
2. What do we need in the Smart Painting Club?

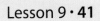

Assessment Test 1

1. Listening

A. Listen, look, and check.

①
a. ☐
b. ☐

② ![]
a. ☐
b. ☐

③
a. ☐
b. ☐

④
a. ☐
b. ☐

⑤
a. ☐
b. ☐

⑥
a. ☐
b. ☐

B. Listen and choose the answer.

1. What does Tom do in his club?
   ⓐ He bakes bread.
   ⓑ He makes movies.

2. Where is the science lab?
   ⓐ It's on the first floor.
   ⓑ It's on the fourth floor.

A. Look and practice the dialog.

A How do you go to school?

B I go to school by bus.

A What's your hobby?

B My hobby is playing soccer.

A What grade are you in?

B I'm in the fifth grade.

A What do you do in your club?

B We make toy robots.

B. Number the sentences in order and practice the dialog.

( ) Alright. I'll turn off the light.

(1) Look at the poster.

( ) Let's save energy.

( ) What's the message of the poster?

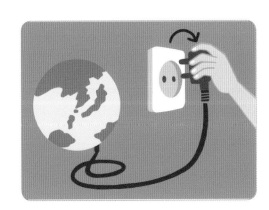

A. **Read and match.**

1. Where is it? •   • a. Yes, he's great.

2. Do you like Sherlock Holmes? •   • b. I'm in the soccer club.

3. Good morning. •   • c. Okay. I won't watch TV.

4. How are you doing? •   • d. It's on the first floor.

5. Which club are you in? •   • e. Good morning.

6. Let's save energy. •   • f. I'm not so good.

B. **Read and check True or False.**

(A) Paula   Does this school have a library?
Bibble   Yes, it does. It's on the second floor.
Paula   What grade are you in?
Bibble   I'm in the fourth grade.
(B) Bibble   What's the message of the poster?
Paula   Let's save energy.
Bibble   Alright! I won't take the elevator.

1. The library is on the fourth floor in this school.   True ☐   False ☐

2. The poster is about saving energy.   True ☐   False ☐

3. Bibble will take the elevator.   True ☐   False ☐

e-learning

A. Choose and write.

| on foot | plant trees | recycle paper | gym |
| music room | bake bread | drawing pictures | fourth |

①
_____

②
_____

③
_____

④
_____

⑤
_____

⑥
_____

⑦
_____

⑧
_____

B. Unscramble the words.

1. **A** What grade are you in?

   B _____
   (I'm / the / second / in / grade / .)

2. **A** What's your hobby?

   B _____
   (pictures / My / is / taking / hobby / .)

3. **A** _____
   (Does / this / computer lab / a / school / have / ?)

   B Yes, it does.

Lesson 11

I'm Watching a Quiz Show

Let's Talk

A. Look, listen, and repeat.

ACT IT OUT

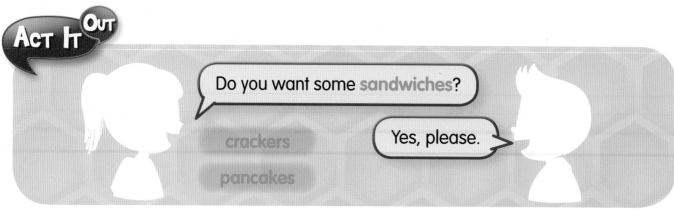

B. Listen and repeat.

I'm watching a **baseball game** .

① baseball game

② comedy

③ music show

④ quiz show

C. Listen, point, and say.

What are you watching?
– I'm watching a _____ .

Let's Learn

A. Listen and chant.

What, what are you watching?

A music show. I'm watching a music show.

Do you want some sandwiches?

Yes, yes, yes, please.

What, what are you watching?

A comedy. I'm watching a comedy.

Do you want some pancakes?

Yes, yes, yes, please.

B. Read, look, and match.

1 A: What are you watching?
B: I'm watching a quiz show.

2 A: What are you watching?
B: I'm watching a comedy.

3 A: What are you watching?
B: I'm watching a music show.

48

A: What are you watching?
B: I'm watching a **cooking show**.

C. Roll the dice. Ask and answer.

① cooking show

② baseball game

③ talk show

④ comedy

⑤ quiz show

⑥ music show

D. Do "Rock-Paper-Scissors.": Ask, answer, and color.

What are you watching?

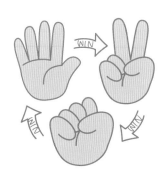

I'm watching a comedy.

TV Programs	comedy	cooking show	talk show	quiz show	music show	baseball game
Points						

Which Girl Is Mandy?

Let's Talk

A. Look, listen, and repeat.

Mom! My friend, Mandy is on TV now.

Which girl is Mandy?

She's the girl with long brown hair.

She's wearing a pink T-shirt.

Oh, I see her.

Thank you.

Today's winner is Mandy. Congratulations!

ACT IT OUT

She's wearing a pink T-shirt.

Oh, I see her.

red coat

yellow dress

B. Listen and repeat.

She's the girl with curly brown hair.

1

curly brown

2

straight red

3

long black

4

short blond

C. Listen, point, and say.

Which girl is _____?
– She's the girl with _____ hair.

1 Jane

2 Stacy

3 Amy

4 Kate

Let's Learn

A. Listen and chant.

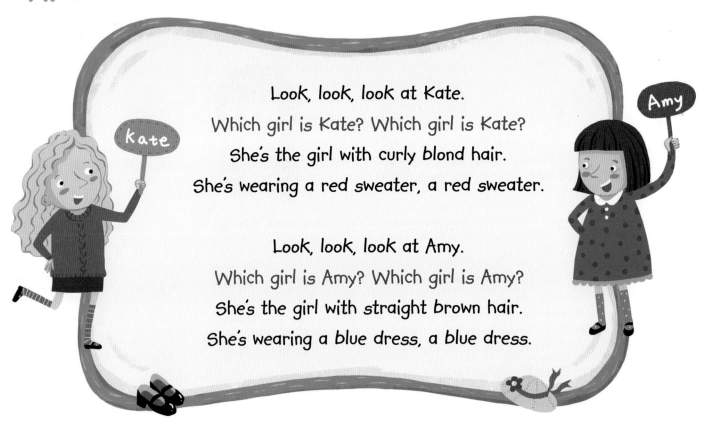

Kate

Look, look, look at Kate.
Which girl is Kate? Which girl is Kate?
She's the girl with curly blond hair.
She's wearing a red sweater, a red sweater.

Look, look, look at Amy.
Which girl is Amy? Which girl is Amy?
She's the girl with straight brown hair.
She's wearing a blue dress, a blue dress.

Amy

B. Listen, look, and number.

C. Look, ask, and answer.

A: Which girl is **Stacy**?
B: She's the girl with **curly black** hair.

① Stacy
curly black

② Kate
short blond

③ Jane
curly brown

④ Grace
straight red

⑤ Cathy
curly blond

⑥ Amy
long black

D. Play the "Ladder Game."

A: Which girl is Katie?
B: She's the girl with curly brown hair.

- Write a girl's name in each box. Then play the game.

Katie

Mrs. Black's Kitchen

A. Look, listen, and repeat.

B. Listen again and write the number in.

1. Oh, Mrs. Black is my mom.
2. I'm watching Mrs. Black's Kitchen.
3. Do you want some crackers?
4. Yes, she's the penguin wearing a red apron.

C. Read and circle True or False.

1. Paula was watching Mr. Black's Kitchen. True False
2. Paula wants to be a cook. True False
3. Bibble has tickets for a movie. True False
4. Mrs. Black is wearing a red apron. True False

D. Do a role-play.

A. Listen and sing.

ON AIR

What Are You Watching?

What are you watching?
I'm watching a cooking show.
Which girl is Jenny?
She's the girl with long black hair.

What are you watching?
I'm watching a quiz show.
Which girl is Cindy?
She's the girl with short red hair.

B. Play a board game.

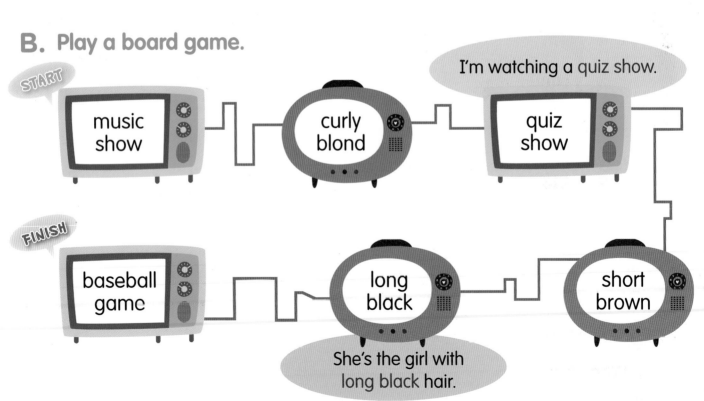

I'm watching a quiz show.

START

music
show

curly
blond

quiz
show

FINISH

baseball
game

long
black

short
brown

She's the girl with
long black hair.

e-learning

Creating Your Own Character

This is my character.
His name is Max.
He's the boy with curly blond hair.
He's wearing a pink shirt and blue pants.

Now, create your own character. It's easy.
Just answer the following questions.
1. What's the name of your character?
2. What hair style does the character have?
3. What's the character wearing?

Name _____

Hair Style _____

Clothes _____

*Draw your character here!

CHECK IT OUT

1. What is Max wearing?

2. What hair style does your character have?

We Need Eggs and Milk

Let's Talk

A. Look, listen, and repeat.

Mandy won first place.

Let's celebrate her victory!

How about making a cake for her?

That's a good idea.

What do we need?

We need eggs and milk.

We need butter and flour, too.

BUTTER

FLOUR

MILK

SUGAR

ACT IT OUT

How about making a cake for her?

buying flowers

singing a song

That's a good idea.

B. Listen and repeat.

We need **butter** .

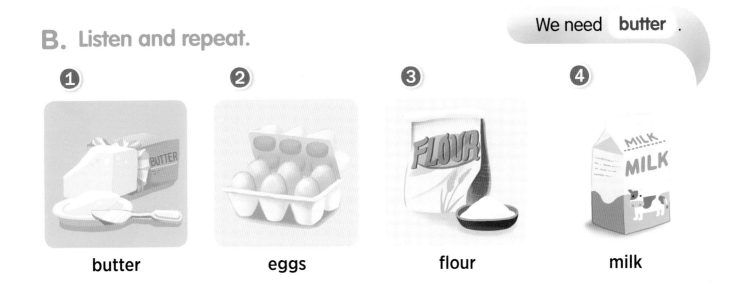

① butter

② eggs

③ flour

④ milk

What do we need?
– We need _____ .

C. Listen, point, and say.

① eggs

② milk

③ butter

④ flour

Let's Learn

A. Listen and chant.

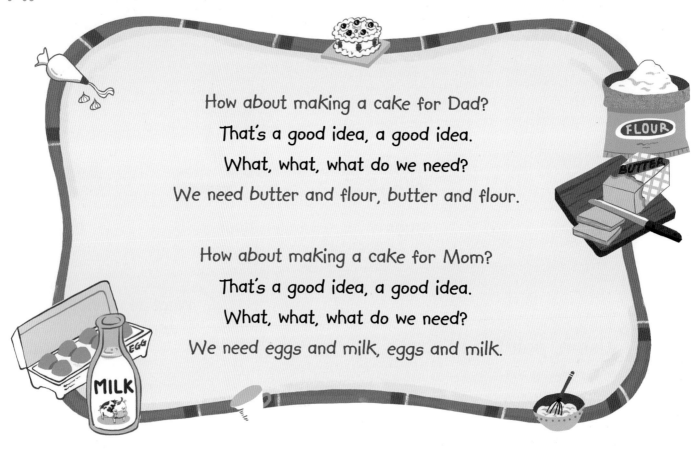

How about making a cake for Dad?

That's a good idea, a good idea.

What, what, what do we need?

We need butter and flour, butter and flour.

How about making a cake for Mom?

That's a good idea, a good idea.

What, what, what do we need?

We need eggs and milk, eggs and milk.

B. Read, look, and choose.

1

A: What do we need?
B: We need flour.

 ⓐ   ⓑ

2

A: What do we need?
B: We need butter.

 ⓐ   ⓑ

3

A: What do we need?
B: We need eggs.

 ⓐ   ⓑ

A: What do we need?
B: We need **milk**.

C. Check. Ask and answer.

① ☐ milk
☐ juice

② ☐ eggs
☐ beans

③ ☐ rice
☐ flour

④ ☐ jam
☐ butter

⑤ ☐ ham
☐ bacon

⑥ ☐ apples
☐ lemons

A: What do we need?
B: We need eggs, oil, and salt.

D. Write. Ask and answer.

Food	Ingredient
fried eggs	eggs, oil, salt

Lesson 15

Let's Put It in the Oven

Let's Talk

A. Look, listen, and repeat.

B. Listen and repeat.

Let's put it in the [blender].

①
blender

②
microwave

③
oven

④
refrigerator

C. Listen, point, and say.

Let's put it in the _____.
– Okay.

Let's Learn

A. Listen and chant.

What's the next step, the next step?
We have to add, add some cheese.
Let's put it in the microwave.
Okay, okay, okay.

What's the next step, the next step?
We have to add, add some water.
Let's put it in the refrigerator.
Okay, okay, okay.

B. Listen, look, and number.

A: Let's put **it (them)** in the **dishwasher**.

B: Okay.

C. Match and talk.

1
it

2
them

3
it

dishwasher

blender

refrigerator

toaster

oven

microwave

4
them

5
it

6
them

A: Let's put the fruit in the refrigerator.
B: Okay.

D. Look and think. Then talk.

fruit

bread

dishes

pizza

salad

A Lemonade Stand

Step Up 5

A. Look, listen, and repeat.

B. Listen again and write the number in.

① What's the next step?

② Did you buy a gift for your mom?

③ We need some lemons, soda water, and honey.

④ Yes, let's sell lemonade.

C. **Read and circle True or False.**

1. This Saturday is Mother's Day. True False
2. Bibble will sell lemonade. True False
3. Bibble and Paula need some milk. True False
4. Bibble and Paula add some honey to the lemonade. True False

D. **Do a role-play.**

A. Listen and sing.

Lemonade and Bread

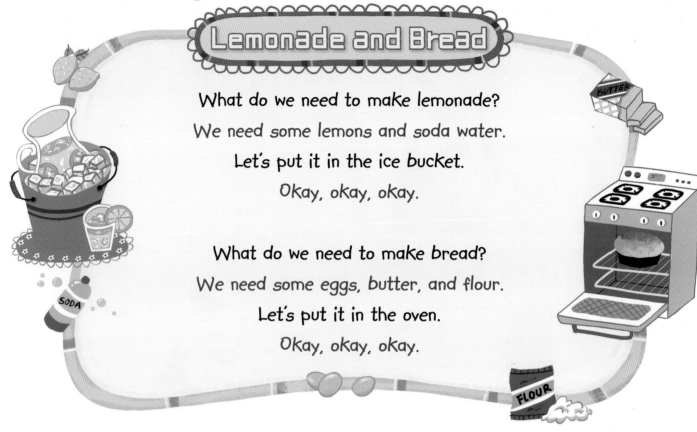

What do we need to make lemonade?

We need some lemons and soda water.

Let's put it in the ice bucket.

Okay, okay, okay.

What do we need to make bread?

We need some eggs, butter, and flour.

Let's put it in the oven.

Okay, okay, okay.

B. Play a board game.

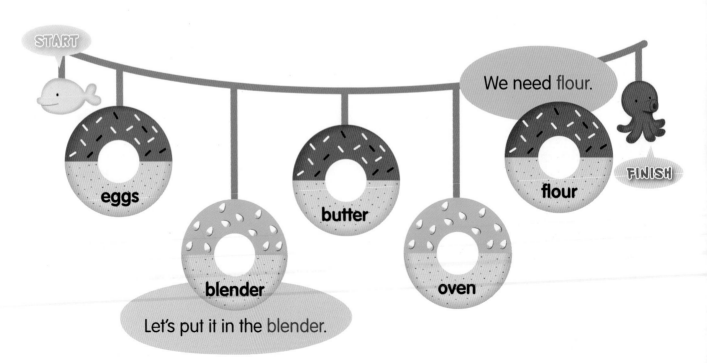

START

We need flour.

eggs

blender

butter

oven

flour

FINISH

Let's put it in the blender.

e-learning

Yummy Tuna Canapés

Ingredients:
1 can of tuna, 1 small onion, mayonnaise, salt, pepper, crackers, a mixing bowl

Steps:
* You have to squeeze the oil out of the tuna before you start.

1. Put the tuna into a mixing bowl.
2. Peel and chop the onion into small pieces.
3. Add mayonnaise, salt, and pepper into the bowl.
4. Mix everything together.
5. Now put the tuna mixture on the crackers.

Tips:
You can add ham and cheese.

CHECK IT OUT

1. What's this recipe for?

2. What's the last step?

Can I Have a Puppy?

Let's Talk

A. Look, listen, and repeat.

Oh, this puppy is so cute.

Mom, can I have a puppy as a pet?

Let's think about it.

I'll take care of it every day.

Well, that's not easy.

Look, Mom! It likes me.

Sorry, Thomas. We can't keep it.

ACT IT OUT

I'll **take care of** it every day.

feed

play with

Well, that's not easy.

B. Listen and repeat.

Can I have a   hamster   as a pet?

①
②
③
④

hamster   hedgehog   parrot   turtle

Can I have a _____ as a pet?
– Let's think about it.

C. Listen, point, and say.

Pet Shop

Let's Learn

A. Listen and chant.

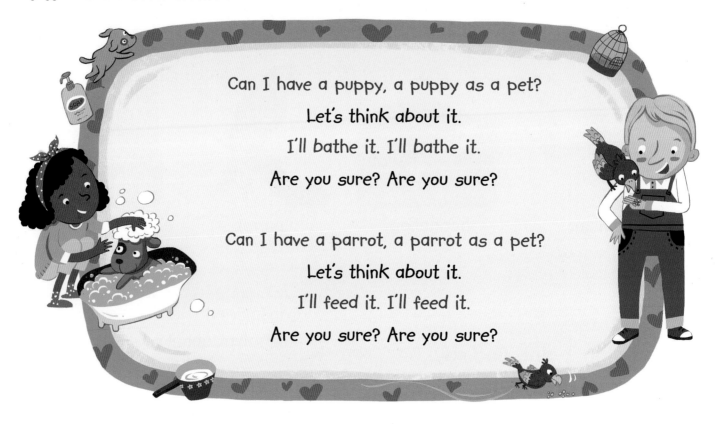

Can I have a puppy, a puppy as a pet?

Let's think about it.

I'll bathe it. I'll bathe it.

Are you sure? Are you sure?

Can I have a parrot, a parrot as a pet?

Let's think about it.

I'll feed it. I'll feed it.

Are you sure? Are you sure?

B. Read, look, and choose.

1 Can I have a puppy as a pet?

ⓐ   ⓑ

2 Can I have a parrot as a pet?

ⓐ   ⓑ

3 Can I have a hamster as a pet?

ⓐ   ⓑ

4 Can I have a turtle as a pet?

ⓐ   ⓑ

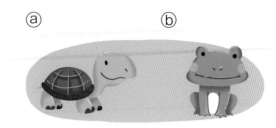

A: Can I have a **puppy** as a pet?
B: Let's think about it.

C. Choose three pets. Ask and answer.

❶   puppy   ❷   hamster   ❸   rabbit

❹   parrot   ❺   turtle   ❻   hedgehog

A: Can I have a hedgehog as a pet?
B: Let's think about it.

D. Play the "Word Strip Bingo."
- Write five words from the word list and play the game.

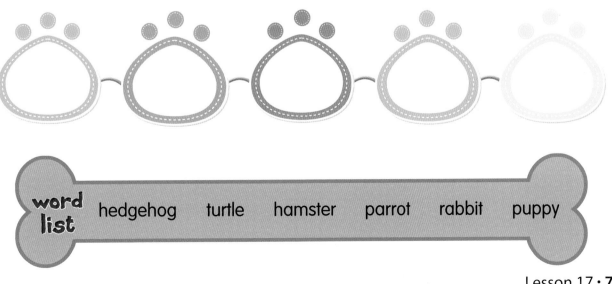

word list   hedgehog   turtle   hamster   parrot   rabbit   puppy

You Must Clean It

A. Look, listen, and repeat.

Thomas, we have a present for you.

What is it?

Thomas' Lab

Look! This lab is for you.

For me? Really?

Are you happy with your lab?

Yes, I am.

You must clean it every day, Thomas.

Okay, I will.

ACT IT OUT

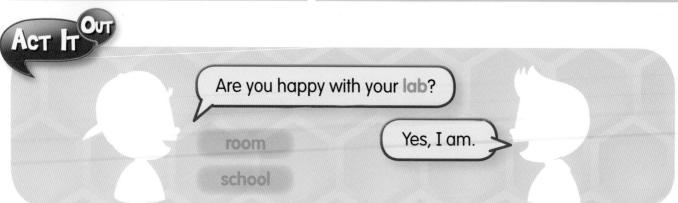

Are you happy with your lab?

room

school

Yes, I am.

B. Listen and repeat.

You must **help older people** .

①

help older people

②

listen to others

③

share with others

④

wait your turn

C. Listen, point, and say.

You must _____ .
– Okay, I will.

Let's Learn

A. Listen and chant.

Are you happy with your room?
Yes, I am. Yes, I am.
You must clean it every day.
Okay, I will. Okay, I will.

Are you happy with your new friends?
Yes, I am. Yes, I am.
You must share with them.
Okay, I will. Okay, I will.

B. Listen, look, and circle.

1. T F
2. T F
3. T F
4. T F

A: You must **wait your turn**.
B: Okay, I will.

C. Match and talk.

1

_____ your turn

2

_____ older people

3

_____ to others

wait   share   help   study   listen   clean

4

_____ with others

5

_____ hard

6

_____ your room

D. Talk and write.

A: You must listen to others.
B: Okay, I will.

• _____listen to others_____

• _____

• _____

• _____

Lesson 19 A Surprise Gift

I'd like a large lemonade, please.

We sold all the lemonade.

Okay, sorry.

SOLD OUT

A. Look, listen, and repeat.

B. Listen again and write the number in.

1 Now, let's go shopping.

2 Mom, I have a gift for you.

3 Excuse me. You must wait your turn.

4 Are you happy with your necklace?

C. **Read and circle True or False.**

1. The seagull cut in line.　　　　　　　　　　　True　　　False
2. Paula and Bibble made some money.　　　　　True　　　False
3. The necklace is 5 dollars.　　　　　　　　　　True　　　False
4. Bibble bought a ring for his mom.　　　　　　True　　　False

D. **Do a role-play.**

A. Listen and sing.

My Pet

Can I have a hedgehog as a pet?
Yes, you can. Yes, you can.
Are you happy with your hedgehog?
Yes, I am. I love it. Thank you.

Can I have a hamster as a pet?
Yes, you can. Yes, you can.
Are you happy with your hamster?
Yes, I am. I love it. Thank you.

B. Play a board game.

START

parrot

Can I have a parrot as a pet?

listen to others

You must wait your turn.

wait your turn

turtle

hedgehog

help older people

Finish

My Pet Happy

My friend Betty has a puppy. The puppy is very cute. I want a puppy, too.

Last week, I asked Mom, "Can I have a puppy as a pet?" She said "Sorry, you can't, Julia." I was very sad.

When I came home from school today, Mom called me. She said, "I have something for you." Amazingly, it was a guinea pig.

I jumped up and down.
"Are you happy with your guinea pig?" Mom asked.
"Yes, I'm very happy. I'm so happy so I'll call her Happy."

guinea pig

I ❤ Happy

CHECK IT OUT

1. What animal does Julia have as a pet?

2. What's the name of Julia's pet?

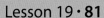

Assessment Test 2

1. Listening

A. Listen, look, and check.

①
a. ☐
b. ☐

②
a. ☐
b. ☐

③
a. ☐
b. ☐

④
a. ☐
b. ☐

⑤
a. ☐
b. ☐

⑥
a. ☐
b. ☐

B. Listen and choose the answer.

1. What do they need?

   ⓐ They need eggs, milk, and flour.

   ⓑ They need eggs, butter, and flour.

2. What is Amy watching?

   ⓐ She's watching a music show.

   ⓑ She's watching a baseball game.

A. Look and practice the dialog.

①

A What do we need?

B We need butter.

②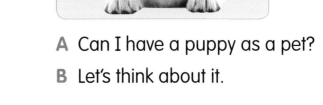

A Can I have a puppy as a pet?

B Let's think about it.

③

A You must help older people.

B Okay, I will.

④

A Let's put it in the microwave.

B Okay.

B. Number the sentences in order and practice the dialog.

◯ Oh, I see her.

◯ Which girl is Bella?

① Look! My friend, Bella is on TV now.

◯ She's the girl with short blond hair.

A. Read and match.

1. How about singing a song for her? •   • **a.** Yes, please.

2. I'll feed it every day.   •   • **b.** Yes, I am.

3. What's the next step?   •   • **c.** Oh, I see her.

4. Do you want some crackers?   •   • **d.** Well, that's not easy.

5. Are you happy with your lab?   •   • **e.** We have to add some salt.

6. She's wearing a pink T-shirt.   •   • **f.** That's a good idea. She'll like it.

B. Read and choose the answer.

(A) Bob   What's the next step for the cake?
Mandy   We have to add some sugar.
Bob   Let's put it in the oven.
Mandy   Okay.

(B) Mom   Are you happy with your lab?
Thomas   Yes, I am.
Mom   You must clean it every day.
Thomas   Okay, I will.

1. Bob will add some _____.
   ⓐ salt   ⓑ sugar

2. Bob and Mandy will put the cake in the _____.
   ⓐ oven   ⓑ microwave

3. Thomas must clean his _____ every day.
   ⓐ lab   ⓑ room

e-learning

A. Choose and write.

butter	curly brown	listen to others	flour
blender	wait your turn	parrot	quiz show

①

_____

②

_____

③

_____

④

_____

⑤

_____

⑥

_____

⑦

_____

⑧

_____

B. Unscramble the words.

1. A _____
(share / must / with / others / You /.)

B Okay, I will.

2. A _____
(put / Let's / in / refrigerator / it / the /.)

B Okay.

3. A _____
(have / as / Can / a hedgehog / a pet / I / ?)

B Let's think about it.

Lesson	Topic	Language	Key Vocabulary
Lesson 1	I'm in the Fourth Grade	What grade are you in? - I'm in the fourth grade. How are you doing? - I'm great.	first second third fourth
Lesson 2	Does This School Have a Library?	Does this school have a library? - Yes, it does. Where is it? - It's on the third floor.	cafeteria gym music room science lab
Lesson 3	A New Friend	Step Up 1 (Review Lessons 1-2) *Reading Time: First Floor vs. Ground Floor	
Lesson 4	How Do You Go to School?	How do you go to school? - I go to school by bike. Good morning. - Good morning.	by bike by bus by subway on foot
Lesson 5	Let's Save Energy	What's the message of the poster? - Let's save energy. I won't take the elevator. - That's great.	plant trees recycle paper save energy save water
Lesson 6	Stop Global Warming	Step Up 2 (Review Lessons 4-5) *Reading Time: Going to School around the World	
Lesson 7	What's Your Hobby?	What's your hobby? - My hobby is reading novels. Do you like Sherlock Holmes? - Yes, he's great.	drawing pictures reading novels riding a bike watching movies
Lesson 8	We Make Toy Robots	What do you do in your club? - We make toy robots. Which club are you in? - I'm in the robot club.	bake bread design clothes make movies make toy robots
Lesson 9	Club Activities	Step Up 3 (Review Lessons 7-8) *Reading Time: New Clubs for You	
Lesson 10	Assessment Test 1 (Review Lessons 1-9)		

Lesson	Topic	Language	Key Vocabulary
Lesson 11	**I'm Watching a Quiz Show**	What are you watching? - I'm watching a quiz show Do you want some sandwiches? - Yes, please.	baseball game comedy music show quiz show
Lesson 12	**Which Girl Is Mandy?**	Which girl is Mandy? - She's the girl with long brown hair. She's wearing a pink T-shirt. - Oh, I see her.	curly brown straight red long black short blond
Lesson 13	Mrs. Black's Kitchen	Step Up 4 (Review Lessons 11-12) *Reading Time: Creating Your Own Character	
Lesson 14	**We Need Eggs and Milk**	What do we need? - We need eggs and milk. How about making a cake for her? - That's a good idea.	butter eggs flour milk
Lesson 15	**Let's Put It in the Oven**	Let's put it in the oven. - Okay. What's the next step? - We have to add some sugar.	blender microwave oven refrigerator
Lesson 16	**A Lemonade Stand**	Step Up 5 (Review Lessons 14-15) *Reading Time: Yummy Tuna Canapés	
Lesson 17	**Can I Have a Puppy?**	Can I have a puppy as a pet? - Let's think about it. I'll take care of it every day. - Well, that's not easy.	hamster hedgehog parrot turtle
Lesson 18	**You Must Clean It**	You must clean it. - Okay, I will. Are you happy with your lab? - Yes, I am.	help older people listen to others share with others wait your turn
Lesson 19	**A Surprise Gift**	Step Up 6 (Review Lessons 17-18) *Reading Time: My Pet Happy	
Lesson 20	**Assessment Test 2**(Review Lessons 11-19)		

Flashcard List

1st	first	2nd	second	3rd	third
4th	fourth		cafeteria		gym
	music room		science lab		by bike
	by bus		by subway		on foot
	plant trees		recycle paper		save energy
	save water		drawing pictures		reading novels
	riding a bike		watching movies		bake bread
	design clothes		make movies		make toy robots
	baseball game		comedy		music show
	quiz show		curly brown		straight red
	long black		short blond		butter
	eggs		flour		milk
	blender		microwave		oven
	refrigerator		hamster		hedgehog
	parrot		turtle		help older people
	listen to others		share with others		wait your turn

Lesson 1 I'm in the Fourth Grade

	Vocabulary	Meaning	Sentence
1	first*	첫 번째의	I'm in the first grade.
2	second*	두 번째의	I'm in the second grade.
3	third*	세 번째의	I'm in the third grade.
4	fourth*	네 번째의	I'm in the fourth grade.
5	fifth	다섯 번째의	I'm in the fifth grade.
6	sixth	여섯 번째의	I'm in the sixth grade.
7	great	매우 좋은	I'm great.
8	fine	좋은	I'm fine.
9	not so good	좋지 않은	I'm not so good.
10	look for	~을 찾다	I'm looking for class 2.
11	grade	학년	What grade are you in?
12	same	같은	We're in the same class.

Lesson 2 Does This School Have a Library?

	Vocabulary	Meaning	Sentence
1	cafeteria*	구내식당	Does this school have a cafeteria?
2	gym*	체육관	Does this school have a gym?
3	music room*	음악실	Does this school have a music room?
4	science lab*	과학 실험실	Does this school have a science lab?
5	library	도서관	Does this school have a library?
6	computer lab	컴퓨터실	Does this school have a computer lab?
7	school	학교	Does this school have a library?
8	where	어디에	Where is it?
9	on	~ (위)에	It's on the third floor.
10	take	데려가다	Let me take you there.
11	there	거기에	Let me take you there.
12	wonderful	멋진	The library is wonderful.

Lesson 5 Let's Save Energy

	Vocabulary	Meaning	Sentence
1	plant trees*	나무를 심다	Let's plant trees.
2	recycle paper*	종이를 재활용하다	Let's recycle paper.
3	save energy*	에너지를 절약하다	Let's save energy.
4	save water*	물을 절약하다	Let's save water.
5	save the Earth	지구를 보호하다	Let's save the Earth.
6	save the sea	바다를 보호하다	Let's save the sea.
7	take the elevator	엘리베이터를 타다	I won't take the elevator.
8	watch TV	TV를 보다	I won't watch TV.
9	use plastic bags	비닐봉지를 사용하다	I won't use plastic bags.
10	minute	분	It only took 10 minutes.
11	poster	포스터	Look at the poster.
12	message	메시지	What's the message of the poster?

Lesson 6 Stop Global Warming (Step Up 2)

	Vocabulary	Meaning	Sentence
1	done	다 끝난	Are you done with your posters?
2	go first	먼저 하다	Do you want to go first?
3	painting	(그림물감으로) 그리는 것	You're good at painting.
4	stop	막다	Let's stop global warming.
5	global warming*	지구 온난화	Let's stop global warming.
6	sea ice	해빙	The sea ice is melting.
7	melt*	녹다	The sea ice is melting.
8	sad	슬픈	I'm sad.
9	here	여기(에), 이곳에	How do the students go to school here?
10	train*	기차	Trams look like trains.
11	jeep*	지프차	Jeepneys look like jeeps.
12	boat*	배	Water buses look like boats.

Lesson 3 A New Friend (Step Up 1)

	Vocabulary	Meaning	Sentence
1	new	새로운	We have a **new** friend here.
2	friend	친구	We have a new **friend** here.
3	meet	만나다	Nice to **meet** you.
4	too	~도 (또한)	Nice to meet you, **too**.
5	brother*	형제	This is my **brother**, Paul.
6	sister*	자매	My **sister** is the same grade as you.
7	as	~처럼 (같이)	My sister is the same grade **as** you.
8	go up*	올라가다	**Go up** one floor and you are on the second floor.
9	floor*	층	Go up one floor and you are on the second **floor**.
10	always	항상	In British English, the same floor is **always** called the ground floor.
11	ground*	지면, 땅	In British English, the same floor is always called the **ground** floor.
12	above	~ 위에	The floor **above** that is the second floor, and so on.

Lesson 4 How Do You Go to School?

	Vocabulary	Meaning	Sentence
1	by bike*	자전거를 타고	I go to school **by bike**.
2	by bus*	버스를 타고	I go to school **by bus**.
3	by subway*	지하철을 타고	I go to school **by subway**.
4	on foot*	도보로	I go to school **on foot**.
5	by car	자동차를 타고	I go to school **by car**.
6	by boat	배를 타고	I go to school **by boat**.
7	morning	아침	Good **morning**.
8	evening	저녁	Good **evening**.
9	night	밤	Good **night**.
10	good at	~을 잘하는	You're **good at** inline skating.
11	how	어떻게	**How** do you go to school?
12	Here we go!	가자!	**Here we go!**

Lesson 7 What's Your Hobby?

	Vocabulary	Meaning	Sentence
1	drawing pictures*	그림을 그리는 것	My hobby is **drawing pictures**.
2	reading novels*	소설을 읽는 것	My hobby is **reading novels**.
3	riding a bike*	자전거를 타는 것	My hobby is **riding a bike**.
4	watching movies*	영화를 보는 것	My hobby is **watching movies**.
5	playing soccer	축구를 하는 것	My hobby is **playing soccer**.
6	taking pictures	사진을 찍는 것	My hobby is **taking pictures**.
7	hobby	취미	What's your **hobby**?
8	these days	요즘에는	What are you reading **these days**?
9	like	좋아하나	Do you **like** Sherlock Holmes?
10	great	굉장한	Yes, he's **great**.
11	hero	영웅	He's my **hero**.
12	board game	보드 게임	Do you like **board games**?

Lesson 8 We Make Toy Robots

	Vocabulary	Meaning	Sentence
1	bake bread*	빵을 굽다	We **bake bread**.
2	design clothes*	옷을 디자인하다	We **design clothes**.
3	make movies*	영화를 만들다	We **make movies**.
4	make toy robots*	장난감 로봇을 만들다	We **make toy robots**.
5	play tennis	테니스를 치다	We **play tennis**.
6	draw cartoons	만화를 그리다	We **draw cartoons**.
7	robot	로봇	I'm in the **robot** club.
8	music	음악	I'm in the **music** club.
9	soccer	축구	I'm in the **soccer** club.
10	meeting	모임	We have a club **meeting** today.
11	reading	독서	Are you in the **reading** club?
12	which	어느(것)	**Which** club are you in?

Lesson 9 Club Activities (Step Up 3)

	Vocabulary	Meaning	Sentence
1	after school	방과 후에	What are you going to do after school?
2	chess	체스	I'm in the chess club.
3	match*	대결, 경기	We have a chess match today.
4	today	오늘	We have a chess match today.
5	join*	가입하다	I didn't join a club yet.
6	yet	아직	I didn't join a club yet.
7	usual*	보통의	In usual sports clubs, students play sports games.
8	sports*	스포츠, 운동	In usual sports clubs, students play sports games.
9	build	조립하다, 건축하다	We build our own robots.
10	tablet PC*	태블릿 PC	In our clubs, we draw and paint pictures with our tablet PCs.
11	need	필요하다	We don't need to buy paper or paint.
12	amazing*	놀라운	It's amazing.

Lesson 11 I'm Watching a Quiz Show

	Vocabulary	Meaning	Sentence
1	baseball game*	야구 경기	I'm watching a baseball game.
2	comedy*	코미디, 희극	I'm watching a comedy.
3	music show*	음악 쇼	I'm watching a music show.
4	quiz show*	퀴즈 쇼	I'm watching a quiz show.
5	cooking show	요리 쇼	I'm watching a cooking show.
6	talk show	토크 쇼	I'm watching a talk show.
7	sandwich	샌드위치	Do you want some sandwiches?
8	cracker	크래커	Do you want some crackers?
9	pancake	팬케이크	Do you want some pancakes?
10	want	원하다	Do you want some sandwiches?
11	hungry	배고픈	I'm hungry.
12	watch	시청하다	I'm watching a quiz show.

Lesson 14 We Need Eggs and Milk

	Vocabulary	Meaning	Sentence
1	butter*	버터	We need butter.
2	egg*	달걀	We need eggs.
3	flour*	밀가루	We need flour.
4	milk*	우유	We need milk.
5	ham	햄	We need ham.
6	lemon	레몬	We need lemons.
7	making a cake	케이크 만드는 것	How about making a cake for her?
8	buying flowers	꽃을 사는 것	How about buying flowers for her?
9	singing a song	노래하는 것	How about singing a song for her?
10	first place	1등	Mandy won first place.
11	celebrate	축하하다	Let's celebrate her victory!
12	victory	승리	Let's celebrate her victory!

Lesson 15 Let's Put It in the Oven

	Vocabulary	Meaning	Sentence
1	blender*	믹서	Let's put it in the blender.
2	microwave*	전자레인지	Let's put it in the microwave.
3	oven*	오븐	Let's put it in the oven.
4	refrigerator*	냉장고	Let's put it in the refrigerator.
5	dishwasher	식기 세척기	Let's put it in the dishwasher.
6	toaster	토스터	Let's put them in the toaster.
7	sugar	설탕	We have to add some sugar.
8	salt	소금	We have to add some salt.
9	pepper	후추	We have to add some pepper.
10	next	다음(의)	What's the next step?
11	add	첨가하다	We have to add some sugar.
12	excited	신 난	I'm so excited.

Lesson 12 Which Girl Is Mandy?

	Vocabulary	Meaning	Sentence
1	curly brown*	곱슬에 갈색의	She's the girl with curly brown hair.
2	straight red*	곧은 빨간색의	She's the girl with straight red hair.
3	long black*	긴 검은색의	She's the girl with long black hair.
4	short blond*	짧은 금발의	She's the girl with short blond hair.
5	curly black	곱슬에 검은색의	She's the girl with curly black hair.
6	curly blond	곱슬에 금발의	She's the girl with curly blond hair.
7	pink T-shirt	분홍색 티셔츠	She's wearing a pink T-shirt.
8	red coat	빨간색 코트	She's wearing a red coat.
9	yellow dress	노란색 드레스	She's wearing a yellow dress.
10	wear	입다	She's wearing a pink T-shirt.
11	see	보이다, 보다	Oh, I see her.
12	winner	우승자	Today's winner is Mandy.

Lesson 13 Mrs. Black's Kitchen (Step Up 4)

	Vocabulary	Meaning	Sentence
1	Mrs.	~ 씨 부인 (결혼한 여성)	I'm watching Mrs. Black's Kitchen.
2	kitchen	부엌	I'm watching Mrs. Black's Kitchen.
3	cook	요리사	I want to be a cook like her.
4	ticket	표	I have tickets for her show.
5	penguin	펭귄	She's the penguin wearing a red apron.
6	apron*	앞치마	She's the penguin wearing a red apron.
7	character	캐릭터	This is my character.
8	boy*	남자아이	He's the boy with curly blond hair.
9	pants*	바지	He's wearing a pink shirt and blue pants.
10	create*	창조하다	Now, create your own character.
11	easy	쉬운	It's easy.
12	question*	질문	Just answer the following questions.

Lesson 16 A Lemonade Stand (Step Up 5)

	Vocabulary	Meaning	Sentence
1	Sunday	일요일	This Sunday is Mother's Day.
2	buy	사다	Did you buy a gift for your mom?
3	gift	선물	Did you buy a gift for your mom?
4	any	어느, 어떤	No, I don't have any money.
5	sell*	팔다	Let's sell lemonade.
6	soda water*	탄산수	We need some lemons, soda water, and honey.
7	honey	꿀	We have to add some honey.
8	ice bucket*	얼음통	Now, let's put it in the ice bucket.
9	squeeze*	짜내다	You have to squeeze the oil out of the tuna before you start.
10	bowl*	(우묵한) 그릇	Put the tuna into a mixing bowl.
11	chop	썰다, 다지다	Peel and chop the onion into small pieces.
12	mayonnaise*	마요네즈	Add mayonnaise, salt, and pepper into the bowl.

Lesson 17 Can I Have a Puppy?

	Vocabulary	Meaning	Sentence
1	hamster*	햄스터	Can I have a hamster as a pet?
2	hedgehog*	고슴도치	Can I have a hedgehog as a pet?
3	parrot*	앵무새	Can I have a parrot as a pet?
4	turtle*	거북이	Can I have a turtle as a pet?
5	puppy	강아지	Can I have a puppy as a pet?
6	rabbit	토끼	Can I have a rabbit as a pet?
7	take care of	돌보다	I'll take care of it every day.
8	feed	먹이를 주다	I'll feed it every day.
9	play with	~와 놀다	I'll play with it every day.
10	have	가지다	Can I have a puppy as a pet?
11	think	생각하다	Let's think about it.
12	keep	(동물을) 기르다	We can't keep it.

Lesson 18 You Must Clean It

	Vocabulary	Meaning	Sentence
1	help older people*	노인을 돕다	You must **help older people**.
2	listen to others*	다른 사람에게 귀를 기울이다	You must **listen to others**.
3	share with others*	다른 사람과 공유하다	You must **share with others**.
4	wait your turn*	너의 차례를 기다리다	You must **wait your turn**.
5	study hard	공부를 열심히 하다	You must **study hard**.
6	clean your room	너의 방을 청소하다	You must **clean your room**.
7	lab	연구실	Are you happy with your **lab**?
8	room	방	Are you happy with your **room**?
9	school	학교	Are you happy with your **school**?
10	present	선물	Thomas, we have a **present** for you.
11	must	~해야 한다	You **must** clean it every day.
12	every day	매일	You must clean it **every day**.

Lesson 19 A Surprise Gift (Step Up 6)

	Vocabulary	Meaning	Sentence
1	large*	(크기가) 큰	I'd like a **large** lemonade, please.
2	Excuse me.	실례합니다.	**Excuse me.**
3	sold*	팔았다	We **sold** all the lemonade.
4	go shopping	쇼핑을 가다	Now, let's **go shopping**.
5	fifteen	15, 열다섯	It's **fifteen** dollars.
6	necklace*	목걸이	Are you happy with your **necklace**?
7	seagull	바다 갈매기	The **seagull** cut in line.
8	cut in line	줄에 새치기하다	The seagull **cut in line**.
9	week*	주	Last **week**, I asked Mom "Can I have a puppy as a pet?"
10	pet*	애완동물	Can I have a puppy as a **pet**?
11	guinea pig*	기니피그	Amazingly, it was a **guinea pig**.
12	call	~라고 부르다	I'll **call** her Happy.

 Memo

 Memo

Answers

Student Book Answers

Reading Time   p. 17
1. It's called the first floor.
2. It's called the first floor.

Lesson 1 I'm in the Fourth Grade
B. Read, look, and match.   p. 8

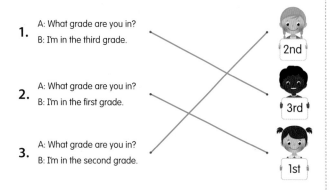

1. A: What grade are you in?
   B: I'm in the third grade.
2. A: What grade are you in?
   B: I'm in the first grade.
3. A: What grade are you in?
   B: I'm in the second grade.

Lesson 4 How Do You Go to School?
B. Look, read, and choose.   p. 20
1. ⓐ   2. ⓑ   3. ⓐ

Lesson 2 Does This School Have a Library?
B. Listen, look, and match.   p. 12

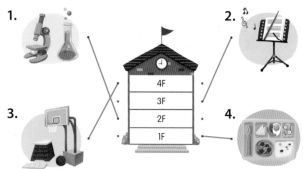

Lesson 5 Let's Save Energy
B. Listen, look, and number.   p. 24

Lesson 3 A New Friend
B. Listen again and write the number in.   p. 14

Lesson 6 Stop Global Warming
B. Listen again and write the number in.   p. 26

C. Read and circle True or False.   p. 27
1. True   2. True   3. False   4. False

Reading Time   p. 29
1. They go to school by Jeepney.
2. They go to school by water bus.

C. Read and circle True or False.   p. 15
1. False   2. False   3. True   4. True

Lesson 7 What's Your Hobby?
B. Read, look, and match. p. 32

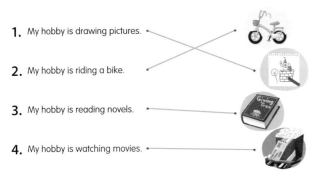

1. My hobby is drawing pictures.
2. My hobby is riding a bike.
3. My hobby is reading novels.
4. My hobby is watching movies.

C. Match. Ask and answer. p. 33

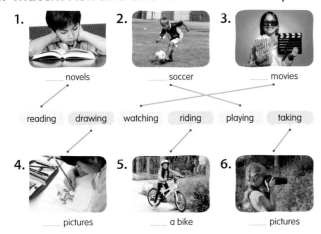

1. _____ novels
2. _____ soccer
3. _____ movies

reading drawing watching riding playing taking

4. _____ pictures
5. _____ a bike
6. _____ pictures

Lesson 8 We Make Toy Robots
B. Listen, look, and circle. p. 36
1. F 2. T 3. F 4. T

Lesson 9 Club Activities
B. Listen again and write the number in. p. 38

C. Read and circle True or False. p. 39
1. True 2. False 3. False 4. True

Reading Time p. 41
1. Robots play soccer games.
2. We need our tablet PCs.

Lesson 10 Assessment Test 1
Listening p. 42
A. 1. a 2. b 3. b 4. a 5. a 6. b
B. 1. ⓐ 2. ⓑ

Speaking p. 43
B. ④ Alright. I'll turn off the light.
   ③ Let's save energy.
   ② What's the message of the poster?

Reading p. 44
A. 1. d 2. a 3. e 4. f 5. b 6. c
B. 1. False 2. True 3. False

Writing p. 45
A. 1. music room 2. drawing pictures
   3. fourth 4. bake bread
   5. plant trees 6. recycle paper
   7. on foot 8. gym

B. 1. I'm in the second grade.
   2. My hobby is taking pictures.
   3. Does this school have a computer lab?

Lesson 11 I'm Watching a Quiz Show
B. Read, look, and match. p. 48

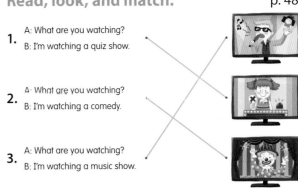

1. A: What are you watching?
   B: I'm watching a quiz show.

2. A: What are you watching?
   B: I'm watching a comedy.

3. A: What are you watching?
   B: I'm watching a music show.

Lesson 12 Which Girl Is Mandy?
B. Listen, look, and number. p. 52

Lesson 13 Mrs. Black's Kitchen
B. Listen again and write the number in.
  p. 54

C. Read and circle True or False. p. 55
1. False 2. True 3. False 4. True

Reading Time p. 57
1. He's wearing a pink shirt and blue pants.
2. [Example] She has long red hair.

Lesson 14 We Need Eggs and Milk
B. Read, look, and choose. p. 60
1. ⓐ 2. ⓑ 3. ⓗ

C. Check. Ask and answer. p. 61
1. milk 2. eggs 3. flour
4. butter 5. ham 6. lemons

Lesson 15 Let's Put It in the Oven
B. Listen, look, and number. p. 64

C. Match and talk. p. 65

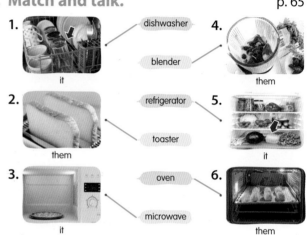

Lesson 16 A Lemonade Stand
B. Listen again and write the number in.
  p. 66

C. Read and circle True or False. p. 67
1. False 2. True 3. False 4. True

Reading Time p. 69
1. It's for tuna canapés.
2. Put the tuna mixture on the crackers.

Lesson 17 Can I Have a Puppy?

B. Read, look, and choose.   p. 72

1. ⓐ   2. ⓑ   3. ⓐ   4. ⓐ

Lesson 18 You Must Clean It

B. Listen, look, and circle.   p. 76

1. T   2. F   3. F   4. T

C. Match and talk.   p. 77

1. _____ your turn
2. _____ older people
3. _____ to others

wait   share   help   study   listen   clean

4. _____ with others
5. _____ hard
6. _____ your room

Lesson 19 A Surprise Gift

B. Listen again and write the number in.

p. 78

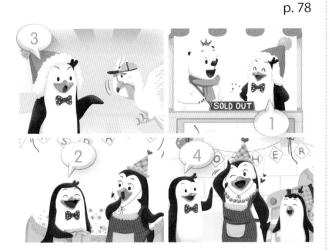

C. Read and circle True or False.   p. 79

1. True   2. True   3. False   4. False

Reading Time   p. 81

1. She has a guinea pig.

2. Her name is Happy.

Lesson 20 Assessment Test 2

Listening   p. 82

A. 1. a   2. b   3. b   4. b   5. a   6. a

B. 1. ⓐ   2. ⓑ

Speaking   p. 83

B. ④ Oh, I see her.

② Which girl is Bella?

③ She's the girl with short blond hair.

Reading   p. 84

A. 1. f   2. d   3. e   4. a   5. b   6. c

B. 1. ⓑ   2. ⓐ   3. ⓐ

Writing   p. 85

A. 1. flour   2. blender

3. quiz show   4. listen to others

5. parrot   6. wail your turn

7. butter   8. curly brown

B. 1. You must share with others.

2. Let's put it in the refrigerator.

3. Can I have a hedgehog as a pet?

Workbook
Answers

Lesson 1 I'm in the Fourth Grade pp. 4~5

A. 2. fourth   3. first   4. third

B. 1. How are you doing?
   2. What grade are you in?

C. 2. doing, fine
   3. How are you doing?
      I'm not so good.

D. 2. are you in, second grade
   3. grade are you in, in the third grade
   4. What grade are you in?
      I'm in the fourth grade.

Lesson 2 Does This School Have a Library?
pp. 6~7

A. 1. cafeteria   2. science lab
   3. gym   4. music room

B. 1. Does this school have a library?
   2. It's on the third floor.

C. 1. fifth
   2. is it, on the third floor
   3. Where is it?
      It's on the second floor.

D. 2. have a library
   3. this school have a cafeteria
   4. Does this school have a science lab?
   5. Does this school have a music room?
   6. Does this school have a computer lab?

Lesson 3 A New Friend   pp. 8~9

A. 1. second   2. fourth
   3. third   4. library
   5. computer lab   6. cafeteria

B. 1. second   2. fourth grade
   3. in the third grade   4. library
   5. have a computer lab
   6. this school have a cafeteria

C. 1. Nice to meet you, too.
   2. Does this school have a cafeteria?
   3. I'm in the second grade.

Lesson 4 How Do You Go to School?
pp. 10~11

A. 1. on foot   2. by subway
   3. by bus   4. by bike

B. 1. Good morning, Thomas.
   2. I go to school by bike.

C. 1. morning
   2. Good evening.
   3. Good night.
      Good night.

D. 2. go to school, to school by bus
   3. do you go to school, go to school by bike
   4. How do you go to school?
      I go to school by subway.

Lesson 5 Let's Save Energy pp. 12~13

A. 1. plant trees   2. save energy
   3. recycle paper   4. save water

B. 1. Let's save energy.
   2. I won't take the elevator.

C. 1. take the elevator
   2. won't use plastic bags, good
   3. I won't watch TV.
      That's good.

D. 2. the poster, save energy
   3. the message of the poster, recycle paper
   4. What's the message of the poster?
      Let's plant trees.

Lesson 6 Stop Global Warming pp. 14~15

A. 1. by bike   2. by bus
3. by subway   4. plant trees
5. save energy   6. save the sea

B. 1. by bike
2. go to school by bus
3. I go to school by subway.
4. plant trees
5. save energy
6. Let's save the sea.

C. 1. You're good at painting.
2. Let's stop global warming.
3. We can go to school on foot.

Lesson 7 What's Your Hobby? pp. 16~17

A.

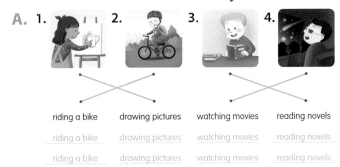

B. 1. My hobby is reading novels.
2. Do you like Sherlock Holmes?

C. 1. Sherlock Holmes
2. like Edison, he's great
3. Do you like Mozart?
    Yes, he's great.

D. 2. hobby, drawing pictures
3. your hobby, is riding a bike
4. What's your hobby?
    My hobby is watching movies.

Lesson 8 We Make Toy Robots pp. 18~19

A. 1. design clothes   2. make movies
3. bake bread   4. make toy robots

B. 1. Which club are you in?
2. What do you do in your club?

C. 1. robot
2. are you in, in the music club
3. club are you in, I'm in the soccer club.

D. 2. design clothes
3. We make movies.
4. We make toy robots.
5. We play tennis.
6. We draw cartoons.

Lesson 9 Club Activities pp. 20~21

A. 1. drawing pictures   2. riding a bike
3. reading novels   4. make toy robots
5. bake bread   6. design clothes

B. 1. is drawing pictures
2. hobby is riding a bike
3. My hobby is watching movies.
4. make movies
5. We play tennis.
6. We draw cartoons.

C. 1. I have a club meeting.
2. Which club are you in?
3. What's your hobby?

Lesson 11 I'm Watching a Quiz Show pp. 22~23

A.

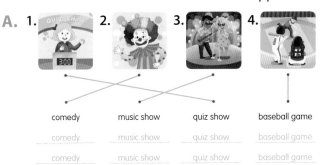

B. 1. Do you want some sandwiches?
2. What are you watching?

C. 1. sandwiches

2. some pancakes, please

3. Do you want some crackers?

Yes, please.

D. 2. you watching, a quiz show

3. are you watching, watching a baseball game

4. What are you watching?

I'm watching a music show.

Lesson 12 Which Girl Is Mandy? pp. 24~25

A. 1. straight red   2. long black

3. short blond   4. curly brown

B. 1. Which girl is Mandy?

2. She's wearing a pink T-shirt.

C. 1. pink T-shirt

2. wearing a yellow dress, I see her

3. She's wearing a red coat.

Oh, I see her.

D. 2. is Kate, with short blond hair

3. girl is Stacy, the girl with curly brown hair

4. Which girl is Amy?

She's the girl with straight red hair.

Lesson 13 Mrs. Black's Kitchen   pp. 26~27

A. 1. music show   2. comedy

3. baseball game   4. short blond

5. curly brown   6. long black

B. 1. a music show

2. watching a quiz show

3. I'm watching a talk show.

4. short blond hair

5. with straight red hair

6. She's the girl with curly brown hair.

C. 1. Do you want some crackers?

2. I'm watching Mrs. Black's Kitchen.

3. Yes, she's the penguin wearing a red apron.

Lesson 14 We need Eggs and Milk

pp. 28~29

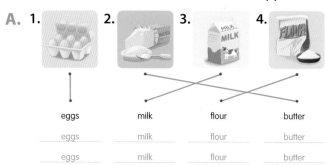

A. 1. eggs   2. milk   3. flour   4. butter

| eggs | milk | flour | butter |
| eggs | milk | flour | butter |

B. 1. How about making a cake for her?

2. What do we need?

C. 1. making a cake

2. about buying flowers for her, a good idea

3. How about singing a song for her?

That's a good idea.

D. 2. we need, need flour

3. do we need, need milk

4. What do we need?

We need butter.

Lesson 15 Let's Put It in the Oven pp. 30~31

A. 1. blender   2. refrigerator

3. microwave   4. oven

B. 1. What's the next step?

2. Let's put it in the oven.

C. 1. sugar

2. the next step, add some salt

3. What's the next step?

We have to add some pepper.

D. 2. in the microwave, Okay.

3. put it in the refrigerator, Okay.

4. Let's put it in the dishwasher.

Okay.

Lesson 16 A Lemonade Stand   pp. 32~33

A. 1. eggs   2. milk   3. lemons

4. refrigerator   5. dishwasher   6. oven

B. 1. milk **2.** eggs **3.** lemons
4. oven **5.** dishwasher **6.** refrigerator

C. 1. Yes, let's sell lemonade.
2. We need some lemons, soda water, and honey.
3. We have to add some honey.

Lesson 17 Can I Have a Puppy? pp. 34~35

A.

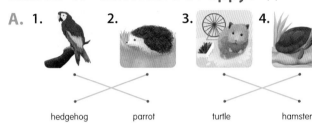

1. 2. 3. 4.

hedgehog parrot turtle hamster

hedgehog parrot turtle hamster

hedgehog parrot turtle hamster

B. 1. Let's think about it.
2. I'll take care of it every day.

C. 1. take care of
2. feed it every day, easy
3. I'll play with it every day.
   that's not easy

D. 2. hamster as a pet
3. have a parrot as a pet
4. I have a turtle as a pet
5. Can I have a rabbit as a pet?
6. Can I have a hedgehog as a pet?

Lesson 18 You Must Clean It pp. 36~37

A. 1. wait your turn **2.** share with others
3. listen to others **4.** help older people

B. 1. Are you happy with your lab?
2. Okay, I will.

C. 1. lab
2. with your room, I am
3. Are you happy with your school?
   I am

D. 2. wait your turn
3. must share with others

4. must help older people
6. You must study hard.
7. You must clean your room.

Lesson 19 A Surprise Gift pp. 38~39

A. 1. hamster **2.** turtle
3. parrot **4.** listen to others
5. help older people **6.** wait your turn

B. 1. hamster
2. a turtle as a pet
3. have a parrot as a pet
4. listen to others
5. must help older people
6. You must wait your turn

C. 1. You must wait your turn.
2. How much is it?
3. Are you happy with your necklace?

Final Test
English Town Book 5

1. ② **2.** ③ **3.** ① **4.** ④ **5.** ③
6. ⑤ **7.** ③ **8.** ⑤ **9.** ② **10.** ④
11. ⑤ **12.** ③ **13.** ④ **14.** ④ **15.** ②
16. ① **17.** bike **18.** pet
19. happy with your room
20. Let's put it in the oven.

Memo

[13-14] Read and answer the questions.

Danny: Look at the poster.
Jenny: What's the message of the poster?
Danny: Let's _____ energy.
Jenny: Alright! I won't take the elevator.
Danny: That's good.

13 What is the right one for the blank?

① do ② use ③ take
④ save ⑤ watch

14 What are they looking at?

① book ② light ③ movie
④ poster ⑤ elevator

[15-16] Read and answer the questions.

Tom: _____
Amy: I'm in the reading club. My hobby is reading novels.
Tom: What are you reading these days?
Amy: I'm reading "Gulliver's Travels."
Tom: Do you like Gulliver?
Amy: Yes, he's great.

15 What is the right one for the blank?

① What's your hobby?
② Which club are you in?
③ What grade are you in?
④ Do you like reading novels?
⑤ What do you do in your club?

16 What is Amy's hobby?

① reading novels ② playing soccer
③ taking pictures ④ drawing pictures
⑤ watching movies

Part 4 - Writing

[17-18] Choose and write the right word.

cat   foot   bike   pet

17

A: How do you go to school?
B: I go to school by _____.

18

A: Can I have a puppy as a _____?
B: Let's think about it.

[19-20] Unscramble and write.

19 A: Are you _____?
B: Yes, I am.

(with / room / your / happy)

20 A: _____
B: Okay.

(put / Let's / in / it / the / oven / .)

Final Test
English Town Book 5

Class	Name	Score
		/20

Part 1 - Listening

[1-2] Listen and choose the right expression.

1

① ② ③ ④ ⑤

2

① ② ③ ④ ⑤

[3-4] Listen and choose the right picture.

3

①   ②   ③

④   ⑤

4

①   ②   ③

④   ⑤

[5-6] Listen and choose the right conversation.

5

① ② ③ ④ ⑤

6

① ② ③ ④ ⑤

Part 2 - Speaking

[7-8] Listen and choose the best response.

7
① I'm tired.   ② Yes, he is.
③ Okay, I will.   ④ I'll try again.
⑤ Sorry, you can't.

8
① I'm shopping.
② I'm cooking pizza.
③ I'm playing a game.
④ I'm reading a novel.
⑤ I'm watching a quiz show.

9 Listen and choose the wrong conversation.

① ② ③ ④ ⑤

10 Listen and choose the best answer to the question.

① ② ③ ④ ⑤

Part 3 - Reading

[11-12] Choose the right one for the blank.

11

> **A:** _____ girl is Grace?
> **B:** She's the girl with short blond hair.

① How   ② Who   ③ What
④ Where   ⑤ Which

12

> **A:** _____
> **B:** We have to add some pepper.

① Where is it?
② What's your hobby?
③ What's the next step?
④ How do you go to school?
⑤ How about making a cake for her?

1 / 2

ENGLiSH TOWN

FOR EVERYONE

BOOK

5

WORKBOOK

YBM

ENGLISH TOWN

FOR
EVERYONE

BOOK
5

WORKBOOK

Contents

I'm in the Fourth Grade

A. Look, check, and write twice.

1
- [ ] sixth
- [✓] second

second

second

2
- [ ] first
- [ ] fourth

_____

_____

3
- [ ] first
- [ ] sixth

_____

_____

4
- [ ] fifth
- [ ] third

_____

_____

B. Choose and write the sentence.

| How are you doing? | What grade are you in? |

1

A _____

B I'm great.

2

A _____

B I'm in the fourth grade.

C. Look and write.

1

great

A How are you doing?

B I'm _____ great _____ .

2

fine

A How are you _____ ?

B I'm _____ .

3

not so good

A _____

B _____

D. Complete the dialogs using the given word.

1. (first) A What grade are you in?

   B I'm in the _____ first _____ grade.

2. (second) A What grade _____ ?

   B I'm in the _____ .

3. (third) A What _____ ?

   B I'm _____ .

4. (fourth) A _____

   B _____

Lesson 2

Does This School Have a Library?

gym   music room
cafeteria   science lab

A. Choose and write twice.

①

②

③

④

B. Choose and write the sentence.

It's on the third floor.

Does this school have a library?

①

A _____

B Yes, it does.

②

A Where is it?

B _____

C. Look and write.

1st floor

① A Where is it?

   B It's on the _____ floor.

② A Where _____ ?

   B It's _____ .

③ A _____

   B _____

D. Complete the questions using the given words.

1. (gym)　　　　　Does this school have a ____gym____ ?

2. (library)　　　Does this school _____ ?

3. (cafeteria)　　Does _____ ?

4. (science lab)　_____

5. (music room)　_____

6. (computer lab)　_____

Lesson **3** **A New Friend**

A. Choose and write.

| third | second | fourth |
| library | cafeteria | computer lab |

 1 2nd

2 4th

3 3rd

_____

4 _____ **5** _____ **6** _____

B. Look at A. Complete the sentences.

1. She's in the _____ grade.

2. He's in the _____ .

3. They're _____ .

4. I like to read books. Does this school have a _____ ?

5. I want to use a computer. Does this school _____ ?

6. I'm hungry. Does _____ ?

C. Can you remember the story? Choose and write.

> I'm in the second grade.

> Does this school have a cafeteria?

> Nice to meet you, too.

A I'm Bibble. Nice to meet you.

B _____

A _____

B Yes, it does. It's on the third floor.

A What grade are you in?

B _____

Reading Time

Read and write.

ground

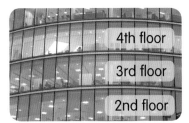

floor

go up

_____

_____

_____

_____

_____

_____

How Do You Go to School?

A. Look, check, and write twice.

① ☐ on foot
☐ by bike
_____
_____

② ☐ by bus
☐ by subway
_____
_____

③ ☐ by car
☐ by bus
_____
_____

④ ☐ by bike
☐ by boat
_____
_____

B. Choose and write the sentence.

| Good morning, Thomas. | I go to school by bike. |

 ①

A _____

B Good morning.

 ②

A How do you go to school?

B _____

C. Look and write.

① morning

A Good morning.

B Good _____ .

② evening

A Good evening.

B _____

③ night

A _____

B _____

D. Complete the dialogs using the given words.

1. (on foot) **A** How do you go to school?

   B I go to school _____ on foot _____ .

2. (by bus) **A** How do you _____ ?

   B I go _____ .

3. (by bike) **A** How _____ ?

   B I _____ .

4. (by subway) **A** _____

   B _____

Let's Save Energy

A. Choose and write twice.

save water   plant trees
recycle paper   save energy

①

_____

_____

②

_____

_____

③

_____

_____

④

_____

_____

B. Choose and write the sentence.

Let's save energy.

I won't take the elevator.

①

A What's the message of the poster?

B _____

②

A _____

B That's good.

C. Look and write.

1

take the elevator

A I won't _____.

B That's good.

2

use plastic bags

A I _____.

B That's _____.

3

watch TV

A _____

B _____

D. Complete the dialogs using the given words.

1. (save water)　**A** What's the message of the poster?

　　　　　　　　B Let's _____ save water _____ .

2. (save energy)　**A** What's the message of _____ ?

　　　　　　　　B Let's _____ .

3. (recycle paper)　**A** What's _____ ?

　　　　　　　　B Let's _____ .

4. (plant trees)　**A** _____

　　　　　　　　B _____

Lesson 6 Stop Global Warming

Step Up 2

A. Choose and write.

| by bus | by bike | by subway |
| plant trees | save the sea | save energy |

① ＿＿＿＿＿＿＿＿＿＿

② ＿＿＿＿＿＿＿＿＿＿

③ ＿＿＿＿＿＿＿＿＿＿

④ ＿＿＿＿＿＿＿＿＿＿

⑤ ＿＿＿＿＿＿＿＿＿＿

⑥ ＿＿＿＿＿＿＿＿＿＿

B. Complete the sentences using the words in A.

1. I have a bike. I go to school ＿＿＿＿＿＿＿＿＿＿＿＿＿＿ .

2. I'm waiting for the school bus. I ＿＿＿＿＿＿＿＿＿＿＿ .

3. The subway is fast. ＿＿＿＿＿＿＿＿＿＿＿＿＿＿＿＿

4. I'll plant some trees tomorrow. Let's ＿＿＿＿＿＿＿＿＿ .

5. I won't take the elevator. Let's ＿＿＿＿＿＿＿＿＿＿ .

6. I won't throw trash in the sea. ＿＿＿＿＿＿＿＿＿＿

14

C. Can you remember the story? Unscramble the words.

A _____

(good / You're / at / painting / .)

B Thank you.

A What's the message of the poster?

B _____

(warming / stop / Let's / global / .)

A What can we do?

B _____

(on / foot / can / We / go / school / to / .)

Reading Time Read and write.

train

jeep

boat

_____

_____

Lesson 7 · What's Your Hobby?

A. Look, match, and write twice.

①

②

③

④

•   •   •   •

•   •   •   •

riding a bike   drawing pictures   watching movies   reading novels

_____   _____   _____   _____

_____   _____   _____   _____

B. Choose and write the sentence.

Do you like Sherlock Holmes?   My hobby is reading novels.

①

A What's your hobby?

B _____

②

A _____

B Yes, he's great.

C. Look and write.

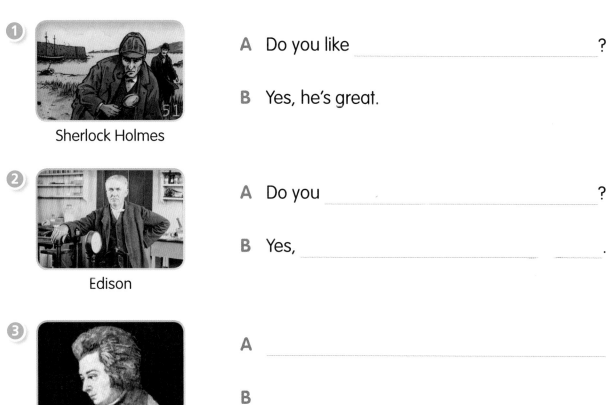

① Sherlock Holmes

A Do you like _____ ?

B Yes, he's great.

② Edison

A Do you _____ ?

B Yes, _____ .

③ Mozart

A _____

B _____

D. Complete the dialogs using the given words.

1. (reading novels) **A** What's your hobby?

   B My hobby is ___ reading novels ___ .

2. (drawing pictures) **A** What's your _____ ?

   B My hobby is _____ .

3. (riding a bike) **A** What's _____ ?

   B My hobby _____ .

4. (watching movies) **A** _____

   B _____

We Make Toy Robots

A. Choose and write twice.

> make movies   bake bread
> design clothes   make toy robots

①

_____

_____

②

_____

_____

③

_____

_____

④

_____

_____

B. Choose and write the sentence.

> What do you do in your club?

> Which club are you in?

①

A _____

B I'm in the robot club.

②

A _____

B We make toy robots.

C. Look and write.

1 robot

A Which club are you in?

B I'm in the _____ club.

2 music

A Which club _____ ?

B I'm _____ _____ .

3 soccer

A Which _____ ?

B _____ _____ .

D. Complete the sentences using the given words.

1. (bake bread)   We _____ bake bread _____ .

2. (design clothes) We _____ .

3. (make movies)   _____

4. (make toy robots) _____

5. (play tennis)   _____

6. (draw cartoons)   _____

Club Activities

A. Choose and write.

> make toy robots   reading novels   design clothes
> drawing pictures   bake bread   riding a bike

① _____

② _____

③ _____

④ _____

⑤ _____

⑥ _____

B. Unscramble the words.

1. My hobby _____ .
   (drawing / is / pictures)

2. My _____ .
   (a / is / hobby / bike / riding)

3. _____
   (hobby / watching / My / is / movies / .)

4. We _____ .
   (movies / make)

5. _____
   (play / We / tennis / .)

6. _____
   (We / cartoons / draw / .)

C. Can you remember the story? Choose and write.

> What's your hobby?

> Which club are you in?

> I have a club meeting.

A What are you going to do after school?

B _____

A _____

B I'm in the chess club.

A _____

B My hobby is baking cakes.

Reading Time   Read and write.

sports

tablet PC

amazing

_____

_____

_____

I'm Watching a Quiz Show

A. Look, match, and write twice.

①    ②    ③    ④

comedy   music show   quiz show   baseball game

_____   _____   _____   _____

_____   _____   _____   _____

B. Choose and write the sentence.

What are you watching?   Do you want some sandwiches?

①

A _____

B Yes, please.

②

A _____

B I'm watching a quiz show.

22

C. Look and write.

1 sandwiches

A Do you want some _____ ?

B Yes, please.

2 pancakes

A Do you want _____ ?

B Yes, _____ _____ .

3 crackers

A _____

B _____ _____

D. Complete the dialogs using the given words.

1. (comedy)

A What are you watching?

B I'm watching a _____ comedy _____ .

2. (quiz show)

A What are _____ ?

B I'm watching _____ .

3. (baseball game)

A What _____ ?

B I'm _____ .

4. (music show)

A _____

B _____

Which Girl Is Mandy?

A. Look, check, and write twice.

☐ straight red
☐ curly brown

_____
_____

② ☐ long black
☐ short brown

_____
_____

③
☐ long blond
☐ short blond

_____
_____

④ ☐ curly red
☐ curly brown

_____
_____

B. Choose and write the sentence.

┌─────────────────────────────┐   ┌─────────────────────────────┐
│ She's wearing a pink T-shirt. │   │   Which girl is Mandy?   │
└─────────────────────────────┘   └─────────────────────────────┘

①

A _____

B She's the girl with long brown hair.

②

A _____

B Oh, I see her.

24

C. Look and write.

1 pink T-shirt

A She's wearing a _____ .

B Oh, I see her.

2 yellow dress

A She's _____ .

B Oh, _____ .

3 red coat

A _____

B _____

D. Complete the dialogs using the given words.

1. (Jane / long black)

A Which girl is _____ Jane _____ ?

B She's the girl with _____ long black _____ hair.

2. (Kate / short blond)

A Which girl _____ ?

B She's the girl _____ .

3. (Stacy / curly brown)

A Which _____ ?

B She's _____ .

4. (Amy / straight red)

A _____

B _____

Mrs. Black's Kitchen

A. Choose and write.

| long black | short blond | curly brown |
| comedy | music show | baseball game |

① ② ③

④ ⑤ ⑥

B. Unscramble the words.

1. I'm watching _____.
   (show / music / a)

2. I'm _____.
   (quiz / show / a / watching)

3. _____
   (I'm / a / talk / watching / show / .)

4. She's the girl with _____.
   (hair / short / blond)

5. She's the girl _____.
   (with / red / hair / straight)

6. _____
   (the / girl / She's / with / curly / hair / brown / .)

26

C. Can you remember the story? Choose and write.

> I'm watching Mrs. Black's Kitchen.

> Do you want some crackers?

> Yes, she's the penguin wearing a red apron.

A _____

B Yes, please.

A What are you watching, Paula?

B _____

A Can you see Mrs. Black?

B _____

Reading Time Read and write.

boy

pants

question

_____ _____ _____

_____ _____ _____

We Need Eggs and Milk

A. Look, match, and write twice.

①	②	③	④

eggs   milk   flour   butter

_____   _____   _____   _____

_____   _____   _____   _____

B. Choose and write the sentence.

What do we need?	How about making a cake for her?

①

A _____

B That's a good idea.

②

A _____

B We need eggs and milk.

C. Look and write.

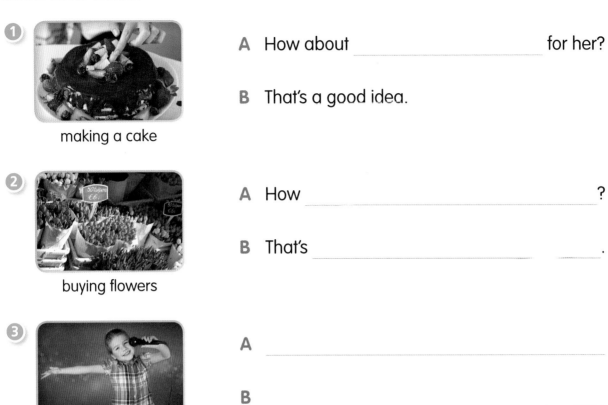

① making a cake

A How about _____ for her?

B That's a good idea.

② buying flowers

A How _____ ?

B That's _____ .

③ singing a song

A _____

B _____

D. Complete the dialogs using the given word.

1. (eggs)   A What do we need?

   B We need _____ *eggs* _____ .

2. (flour)   A What do _____ ?

   B We _____ .

3. (milk)   A What _____ ?

   B We _____ .

4. (butter)   A _____

   B _____

15 Let's Put It in the Oven

A. Look, check, and write twice.

1
☐ blender
☐ dishwasher

_____
_____

2
☐ microwave
☐ refrigerator

_____
_____

3
☐ toaster
☐ microwave

_____
_____

4
☐ oven
☐ dishwasher

_____
_____

B. Choose and write the sentence.

⟮ What's the next step? ⟯   ⟮ Let's put it in the oven. ⟯

1

A _____

B We have to add some sugar.

2

A _____

B Okay.

C. Look and write.

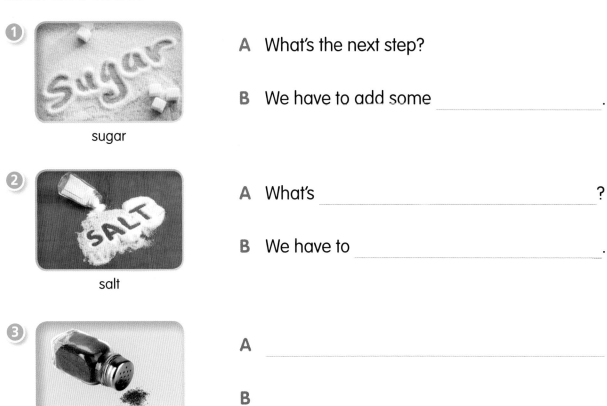

① sugar

A What's the next step?

B We have to add some _____.

② salt

A What's _____?

B We have to _____.

③ pepper

A _____

B _____

D. Complete the dialogs using the given word.

1. (toaster) **A** Let's put it in the ____toaster____.

   B Okay.

2. (microwave) **A** Let's put it _____.

   B _____

3. (refrigerator) **A** Let's _____.

   B _____

4. (dishwasher) **A** _____

   B _____

 Step Up 5

A Lemonade Stand

A. Choose and write.

> milk   lemons   eggs
> dishwasher   oven   refrigerator

1

_____

2

_____

3

_____

4

_____

5

_____

6

_____

B. Complete the sentences using the words in A.

1. Let's make milkshake. We need _____ .

2. Let's make fried eggs. We need _____ .

3. Let's make lemonade. We need _____ .

4. Let's put the pizza in the _____ .

5. Let's put the dishes in the _____ .

6. Let's put the vegetables in the _____ .

C. Can you remember the story? Unscramble the words.

A We can make some money.

B _____

(let's / Yes, / lemonade / sell / .)

A What do we need?

B _____

(and honey / some lemons, soda water, / need / We / .)

A What's the next step?

B _____

(add / have / some / to / We / honey / .)

Reading Time Read and write.

mayonnaise

bowl

squeeze

_____   _____   _____

_____   _____   _____

Can I Have a Puppy?

A. Look, match, and write twice.

①
②
③
④

hedgehog   parrot   turtle   hamster

_____   _____   _____   _____

_____   _____   _____   _____

B. Choose and write the sentence.

> I'll take care of it every day.   Let's think about it.

①

A   Can I have a puppy as a pet?

B   _____

②

A   _____

B   Well, that's not easy.

C. Look and write.

①

take care of

A I'll _____ it every day.

B Well, that's not easy.

②

feed

A I'll _____ .

B Well, that's not _____ .

③

play with

A _____

B Well, _____ .

D. Complete the sentences using the given word.

1. (puppy)   Can I have a _____ puppy _____ as a pet?

2. (hamster)   Can I have a _____ ?

3. (parrot)   Can I _____ ?

4. (turtle)   Can _____ ?

5. (rabbit)   _____

6. (hedgehog)   _____

You Must Clean It

A. Choose and write twice.

help older people   wait your turn
listen to others   share with others

_____

_____

_____

_____

_____

_____

_____

_____

B. Choose and write the sentence.

Okay, I will.   Are you happy with your lab?

A _____

B Yes, I am.

A You must clean it every day, Thomas.

B _____

C. Look and write.

1

lab

A Are you happy with your _____ ?

B Yes, I am.

2

room

A Are you happy _____ ?

B Yes, _____ .

3

school

A _____

B Yes, _____ .

D. Complete the sentences using the given words.

1. (listen to others)　　You must ___listen to others___ .

2. (wait your turn)　　You must _____ .

3. (share with others)　　You _____ .

4. (help older people)　　You _____ .

5. (study hard)　　_____

6. (clean your room)　　_____

Lesson 19 A Surprise Gift

A. Choose and write.

hamster   parrot   help older people
turtle   wait your turn   listen to others

_____

_____

_____

_____

_____

_____

B. Complete the sentences using the words in A.

1. It looks like a mouse. Can I have a _____ as a pet?

2. It lives long. Can I have _____?

3. I like birds. Can I _____?

4. You must _____ more carefully.

5. You _____ in need.

6. _____ in line.

C. Can you remember the story? Unscramble the words.

A _____
(must / You / turn / your / wait / .)

B Okay, sorry.

A _____
(it / is / How / much / ?)

B It's fifteen dollars.

A _____
(you / Are / happy / your / necklace / with / ?)

B Yes, I am. I love it.

Reading Time Read and write.

week

pet

guinea pig

_____

_____

_____

Memo

ENGLiSH TOWN

BOOK 5

ENGLiSH TOWN BOOK 5

English Town is a spoken English course comprised of a series of 9 books, specifically designed for elementary school students.

- Learning English in a communicative way and in an easy manner
- Focused approach to new words, expressions, and dialogs
- Fun to sing and chant together
- Simple but effective games and activities
- Exciting stories

Components

· Student Book

· Workbook

· Final Test

· Teacher's Guide including teaching resources

· Online (www.ybmenglishtown.com)

  Interactive e-book for teachers and students

  E-learning for self-study

 www.ybmenglishtown.com

YBM